MINECRAFT

MASTER BUILDER

DINOSAURS

THIS IS A MORTIMER CHILDREN'S BOOK

Text, design and illustration © Welbeck Children's Limited 2020

Published in 2020 by Mortimer Children's Limited
An imprint of the Welbeck Publishing Group
20 Mortimer Street, London W1T 3JW

This book is not endorsed by Mojang Synergies AB. Minecraft and
Minecraft character names are trademarks of Mojang Synergies AB.
All screenshots and images of Minecraft characters/gameplay
© Mojang Synergies AB.

Dinosaurs built by:
Ben Westwood

The publishers would like to thank the following sources for their kind
permission to reproduce the pictures in this book.

ALAMY: /Roberto Nistri: 72C; /Stocktrek Images, Inc.: 8R, 9TL, 9R

SHUTTERSTOCK: /Ton Bangkeaw: 41T; /Catmando: 7TR, 9BL, 72B; /Pavel
Chagochkin: 4TR; /DM7: 40R; /Dotted Yeti: 56B; /Elenarts: 57TR; /Daniel
Eskridge: 5TR, 7B, 24C, 24-25, 25T; /Jean-Michel Girard: 41BR, 57L; /Natalia
Gorbach: 56R; /Herschel Hoffmeyer: 6BL, 25C; /Matis75: 41L; /Michael
Rosskothen: 8B, 57BR; /Warpaint: 6BR; /YuRi Photolife: 40BL

A catalogue record for this book is available from the British Library.

ISBN: 978 1 83935 001 6

Printed in China
1 3 5 7 9 10 8 6 4 2

Designed, written and packaged by: Dynamo Limited
Design Manager: Emily Clarke
Editorial Manager: Joff Brown
Production: Nicola Davey

MINECRAFT

MASTER BUILDER

DINOSAURS

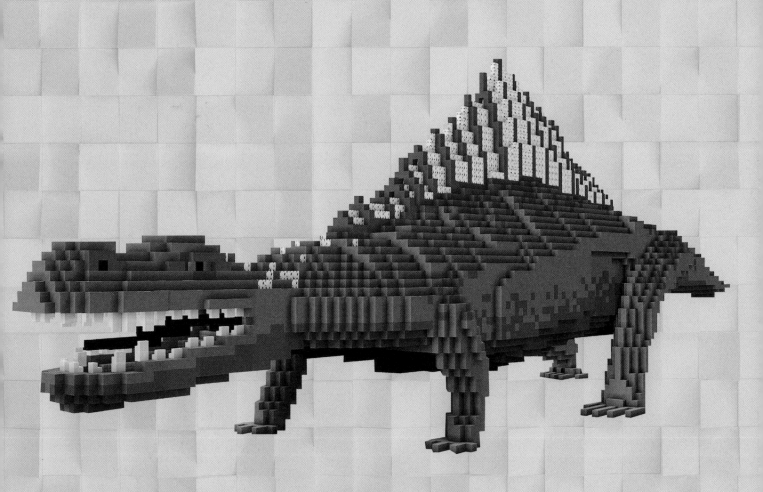

MORTIMER

CONTENTS

PTERODACTYL

EORAPTOR

ALLOSAURUS

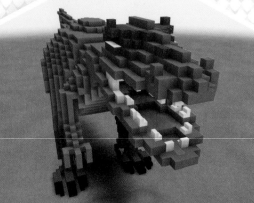

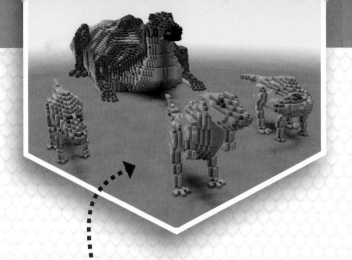

MAIASAURA

STEGOSAURUS

ANKYLOSAURUS

TRICERATOPS

WELCOME TO MINECRAFT
≪ DINOSAURS ≫

This book is your one-stop guide to building heaps of incredible dinosaurs. Inside you'll discover creatures who roamed the land, sea and sky for 150 million years. We'll journey back in time through the Mesozoic Era. We'll explore the Triassic to the Jurassic, right up to the Cretaceous period. Plus, you'll get to know your Allosaurus from your Diplodocus, and your Brachiosaurus from your mighty Mosasaurus! Let's do this.

 ## NEW TO MINECRAFT?

If you are yet to experience the joys of Minecraft, then you're in for a big treat! It's a good idea to familiarise yourself with the way things work before you get stuck into building. Play around with the basic game play to see what you can do. If you take some time to get to grips with Minecraft, the more fun you'll have when it's time to get creative.

 ## DOING MORE

This book has a great selection of super-cool prehistoric creatures, but why stop there? Once you've polished up your Minecraft skills using our step-by-steps, you can have a go at building any dinosaurs you fancy. You could even come up with your own dinosaurs! How about merging a T. rex with a flying Pterodactyl? Or, take your dino builds to the next level by creating a whole prehistoric land for them to live in. The possibilities are endless!

ARCHAEOPTERYX

ANKYLOSAURUS

STAYING SAFE ONLINE

Minecraft is one of the best games on the planet because it combines amazing building skills with having fun! However, the most important part of the game is to stay safe when you're online.

Below are our tips for keeping safe:

- ❏ tell a trusted adult what you're doing and ask before downloading anything

- ❏ speak to a trusted adult if you are worried about anything

- ❏ turn off chat

- ❏ find a child-friendly server

- ❏ only screenshare with real-life friends

- ❏ watch out for viruses and malware

- ❏ set a game-play time limit

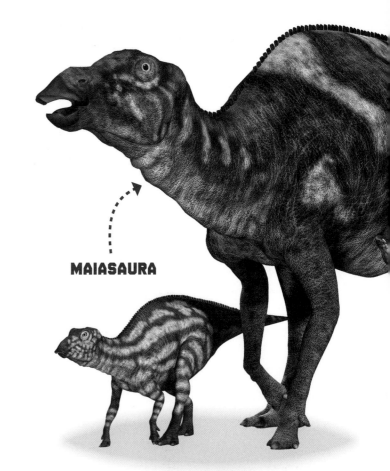

MAIASAURA

BRACHIOSAURUS

TERRIFIC
« TRIASSIC »

We're kicking things off in the Triassic period, which was about 250 to 200 million years ago. It was during the Triassic period that dinosaurs first appeared on the Earth, but things looked pretty different back then. For starters, all of the continents were connected in one giant landmass known as Pangea. Conditions were harsh, as it was mainly desert, so you had to be tough to survive. What kind of dinosaurs roamed the land during this time? Let's find out.

 ## EORAPTOR

You might not have heard of an Eoraptor. These small theropods were about one metre long, and they were one of the very first dinosaurs to roam the Earth. Speedy Eoraptors raced around on two legs and had large clawed hands for grabbing prey. Their jaws had a combination of rounded and super-sharp teeth, which were ideal for feasting on both plants and animals.

 ## ARIZONASAURUS

Including the fin on its back, this dinosaur came in at roughly the same height as a Great Dane – but it was three times as long. That's one huge pet! As you might have guessed from its name, this dinosaur roamed the area that is now known as Arizona, in the United States.

Not much is known about this small, meat-eating theropod as only parts of its skeleton have been found. Its name means 'hopping foot' and it would have been found hopping around Scotland between 210 and 221 million years ago.

⟪ HERRERASAURUS ⟫

The Herrerasaurus lived during the late Triassic Period. Its name means 'Herrera's lizard' after the person that first discovered a fossil of it. At three metres long, these theropods were the biggest predators of their time. Yikes! They were known for their flexible jaws, which could slide backwards and forwards to trap their prey.

The first **Herrerasaurus** fossils were found in the 1960s.

⟪ PLATEOSAURUS ⟫

The epic Plateosaurus could grow up to around eight metres in length. Their bones were much thicker and stronger than most other dinos of this era. Plateosauruses were herbivores and walked on either two or four legs. Their long flexible necks meant that they could reach the high up branches that other species couldn't get to. Pretty nifty, eh?

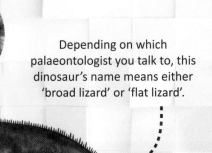

Depending on which palaeontologist you talk to, this dinosaur's name means either 'broad lizard' or 'flat lizard'.

Plateosaurus fossils were some of the first dinosaur fossils found. And now over 100 different skeletons have been dug up.

EORAPTOR

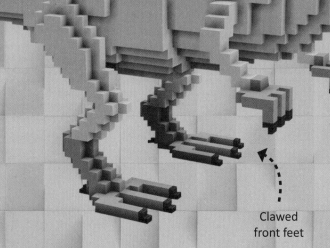

These dinky dinos weighed around 200kg

Eoraptors sped around on their hind legs and were small, fierce hunters! Now, it's your turn to build one...

Clawed front feet

MATERIALS

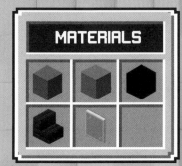

STEP 1

Begin with brown blocks to create a foot with three claws. Then, use grey blocks to build the leg. Give it a slightly bent knee, like this. Repeat this to build the second leg.

STEP 2

Now it's time to connect the two legs by creating an oval of grey blocks. This oval will help you to shape the torso later on.

STEP 3

Use this picture to help you build the net of the Eoraptor's body from grey blocks. Give it a smooth, curved neck at the front and a pointed tail at the back.

STEP 4

Create rings along the length of the torso with grey blocks. The middle of the torso should have the largest rings,= as this will shape the stomach.

STEP 5

Look at the picture for how to fill in the tail. Make it thinner as you get closer to the tip, ending in a single layer.

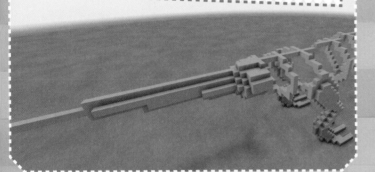

STEP 6

Now it's time to fill in the torso to make it into a solid shape. Add the grey blocks in layers to create a rounded look for your dinosaur's body.

STEP 7

Next, move onto the Eoraptor's neck. Have a go at making this a solid shape, too. Don't worry about making it 3D just yet.

STEP 8

Build a frame for the face and beak using grey and brown blocks. Play around until you're happy with the shape.

STEP 9

Build up the face, as shown here. Use black blocks for the eyes and more brown blocks to make the beak.

STEP 10

You'll need some more brown blocks for the underside of the beak. This is what your dino's face should now look like from below.

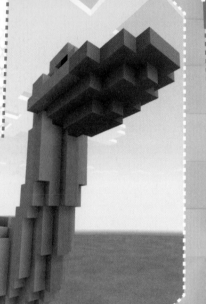

STEP 11

Use grey blocks to create a front leg on each side of the torso. Eoraptors had pretty short front legs, so you won't need many grey blocks for this bit!

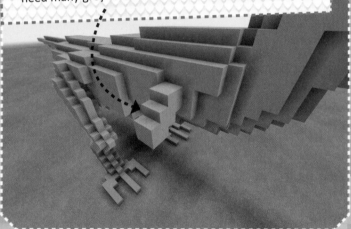

STEP 12

Finally, add some clawed brown front feet. They should be slightly smaller than the ones you created in step 1. Take a look at the picture to see how we curled the claws over to make the Eoraptor's grabbing hands!

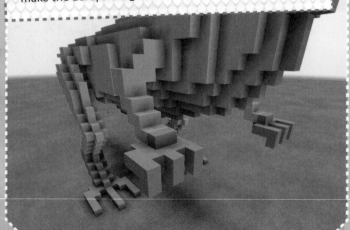

STEP 13

Add dark brown blocks to the front and back claws. Your Eoraptor is complete!

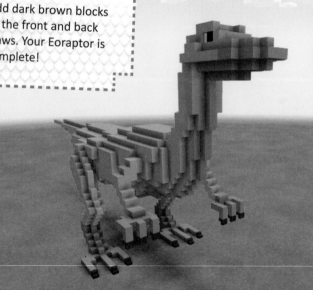

PLATEOSAURUS

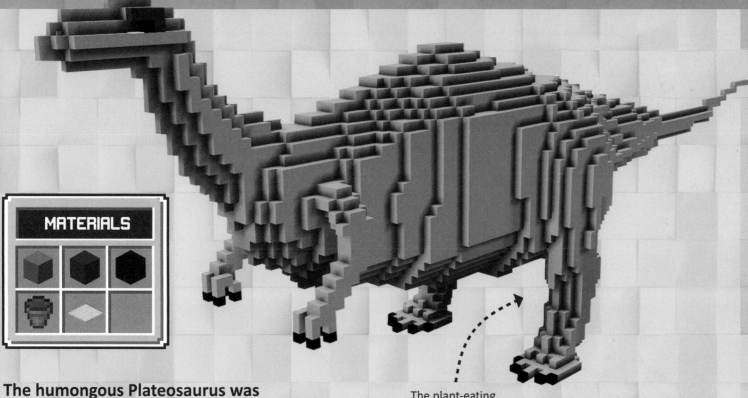

MATERIALS

The humongous Plateosaurus was one of the first dino fossils to be discovered. So, blocks at the ready and let's build one!

The plant-eating **Plateosaurus** walked about on its two hind legs.

STEP 1

Begin by creating a large orange foot with five toes, like this. Don't forget to give it some fierce black claws.

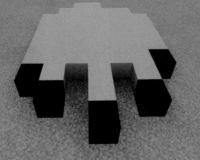

STEP 2

Continue using orange blocks to build up the bottom half of the leg. Check out the picture to help you get the shape just right.

STEP 3

For the top of the leg, create a loop of orange blocks, as shown. This bit should be wider than the lower leg you built in steps 1 and 2.

STEP 4

Now, it's time to fill in the loop. Have a go at building up layers of orange blocks to give it a 3D effect. Each layer should be slightly smaller than the one underneath.

STEP 5

Repeat these steps to create a second leg. Add a row of curved orange blocks to connect the two together.

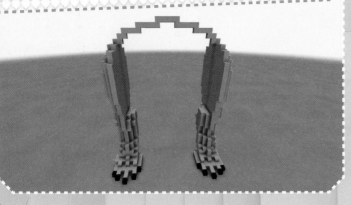

STEP 6

Use the below image to help you create your dino's spine. The tail will be at the end, and the head shape at the front.

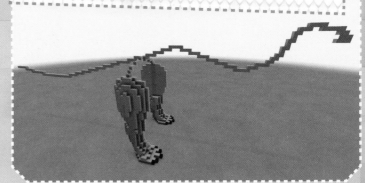

STEP 7

Build a second row of orange blocks underneath this one. Be sure to give your Plateosaurus a pointy tail and a rounded stomach.

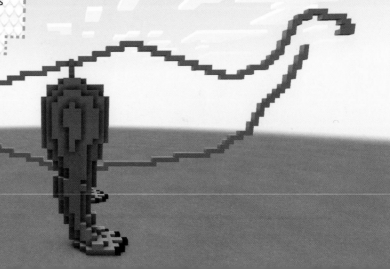

STEP 8

Next, create a net for its tail. Make it super wide at the end closest to the body, forming a thin tip at the end.

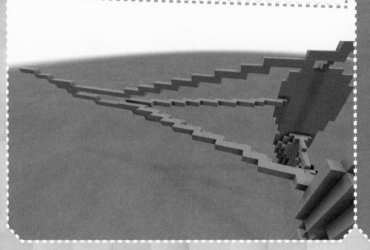
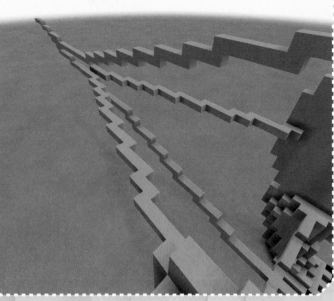

STEP 9

When you're happy with the tail and body frame, fill in the top half of the torso. Try overlapping the blocks in steps, like this.

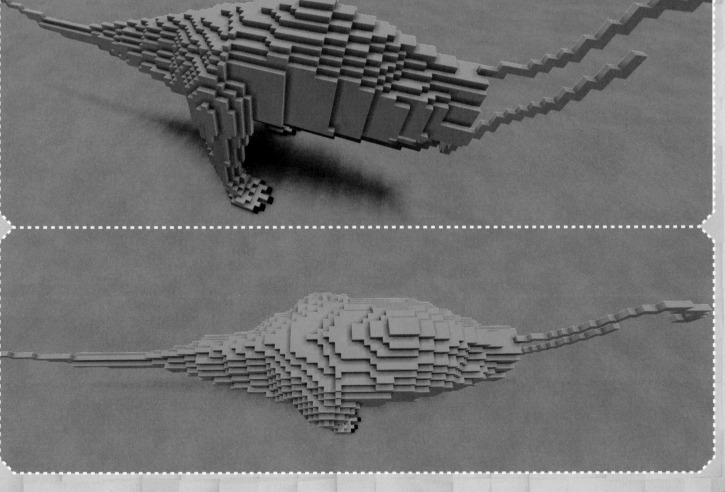

STEP 10

Fill in the neck to make it a solid shape, like this. This is your chance to check that you're happy with the head shape and size.

STEP 11

Your build should now look like this from the side. Now you can begin filling in the underside of your dino.

STEP 12

Add stumps for arms at the front of the torso. It should look a bit like this picture. Check out step 18 to help you figure out where they go!

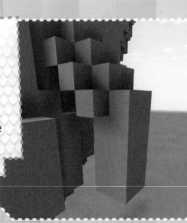

STEP 13

Keep adding to the arms to make them curve out in front of the torso. You won't need many blocks for this dino's small arms!

STEP 14

Complete the arms by giving them fingers with claws made from black blocks – just like the ones you made in step 1.

STEP 15

Next, use more orange blocks to shape the bottom part of the head. Yours should look a bit like the one below.

STEP 16

Use rows of orange blocks to fill in your dino's head so that it becomes a solid, 3D shape.

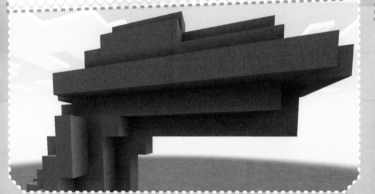

STEP 17

Bring your dino to life with black eyes. Use a few dark brown blocks to frame them. We added a yellow block in front of each eye to make it pop! Finally add two red nostrils.

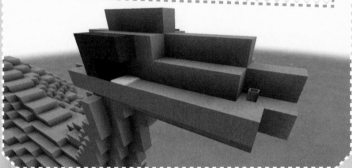

STEP 18

Hooray, your dino is done! Take a moment to make any tweaks, then sit back and admire your building skills.

ARIZONASAURUS

Push your building skills to the max with the super spiny Arizonasaurus!

The sail along its back might have been used to regulate the **Arizonasaurus'** body. temperature

STEP 1

Get your grey blocks ready to build this dino's five-toed back foot. Try to make the shape of its heel just like the image below.

STEP 2

Look closely at this two-step guide for creating the leg. It should be leaning backwards slightly. First, create the outline, then fill it in.

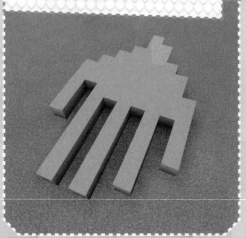

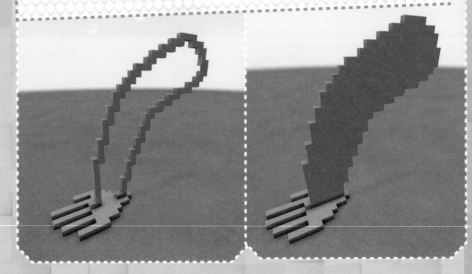

STEP 3

Layer up the blocks to make the leg a 3D shape. Add in a row of grey blocks for hips, as shown below. The length should be the width of your dino's torso.

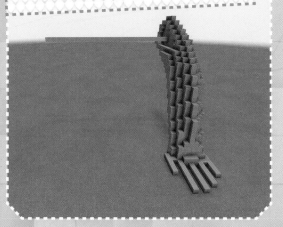

STEP 4

The second leg will be shaped differently, to show that your dinosaur is walking. Use this picture as a guide for how to create the shape.

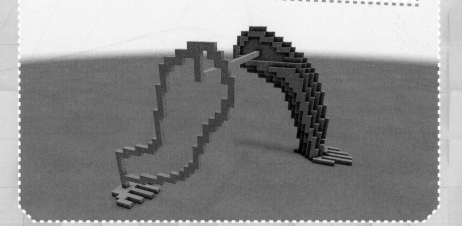

STEP 5

Once you have made the shape of your second back leg, you can pad it out with plenty of grey blocks to make it 3D.

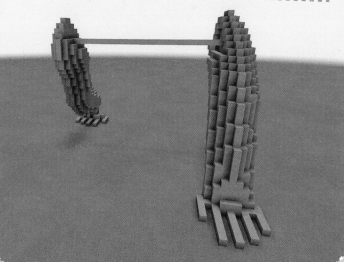

STEP 6

Build forwards from the legs to make a frame for the torso. Make two indents to create spaces for the two front legs.

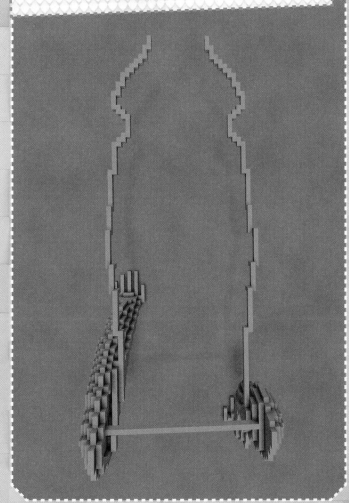

STEP 7

At the back of the dino's torso, add in an arch that reaches from one leg to the other. It should be built just above the row of blocks that you added in Step 5.

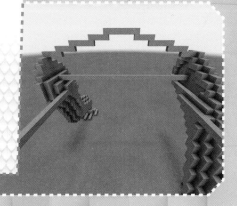

STEP 8

For the next step, build a row of blocks to give your dino its back and spine. This is how your dinosaur should look from the side.

STEP 9

Slot two front leg outlines into the indents you built into the torso. The front legs should be the same shape as the back ones, but a little smaller.

STEP 10

Use grey blocks to make the front legs 3D. Notice how the front legs match each other, rather than being in a walking position.

STEP 11

Create a circular shape at one end of the torso, just in front of the two front legs. It should come just in front of the two front legs. This is the start of your dinosaur's neck and head.

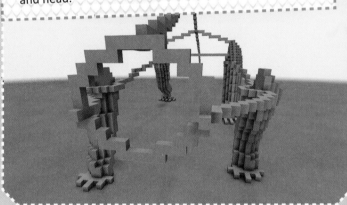

STEP 12

For the underside of your dino's torso, build a curved strip of grey blocks down the centre of your build. It should join up the circle (Step 11) with the hips (Step 3).

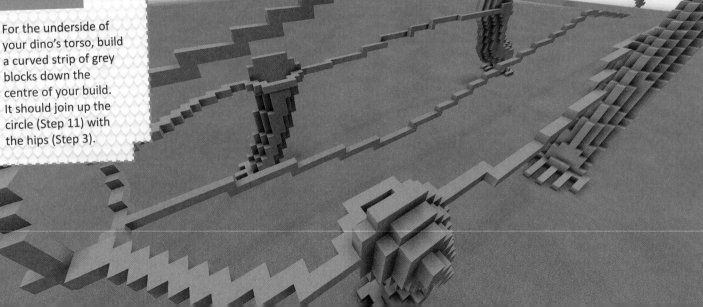

STEP 13

Now that the frame of the torso is done, it's time to fill it in. Take a moment to look at the picture below to see how we have added layers to create a 3D shape.

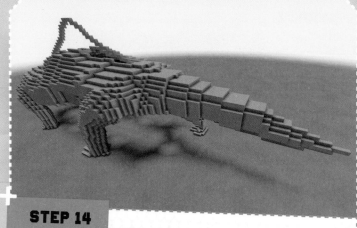

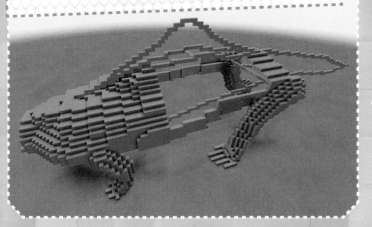

STEP 14

Apart from the sail, the dino's torso should now be entirely filled in. Make the tail thinner as you reach the tip to make it look like a real Arizonasaurus!

STEP 15

Drop in some dark green blocks to decorate the legs, as shown in the picture. You can use as many as you like. Try out this technique on the top of each leg.

STEP 16

To make the sail, start by adding two rows of green blocks around the base. Your dino should now look like this.

STEP 17

To build the spines, create arches of green blocks along the length of the sail. Then, add pale grey or white blocks to fill the spaces between the spines. It should end up looking like the second image here.

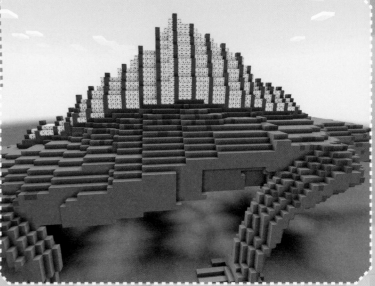

STEP 18

Your Arizonasaurus is missing its tummy! Layer up green blocks to create a rounded underside. Leave some gaps between your blocks so that you can overlap the two colours to form a colour gradient.

This is how the gradient should look when it's complete.

STEP 19

The final part of your build is the face. Start with an oval-shaped upper jaw, and then add a line of blocks in an arched shape to create the top of its head. The arch should have two peaks, as in the picture on the right.

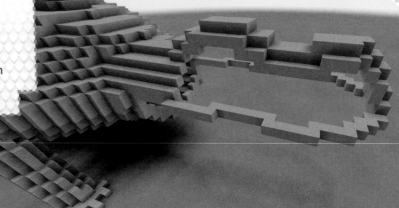

STEP 20

Fill in the face shape using a combination of grey and green blocks. Create two large nostrils, plus two glowing orange eyes. Frame both eyes with a few green blocks so that they really pop!

STEP 21

Next, build the bottom jaw, like this. Make sure its mouth is open to show off the heaps of big teeth that you'll add in the following steps!

STEP 22

Use a line of dark pink blocks for the gums and a paler pink for the rest of the mouth. Create a tongue using black bricks.

STEP 23

All you need now are some white blocks to give your dino some chomp-tastic teeth. Leave a gap between each tooth to give them definition.

STEP 24

Finally, add a few pale blocks as decoration to the area around the dino's shoulders and the back of its head. Arizonasaurus, done!

GIGANTIC
« JURASSIC »

The Jurassic era took place 200 to 145 million years ago, when the world's landmass began to break apart. This is the time when the landscape and climate of Earth changed dramatically, bringing with it more rainfall and plant life. It makes sense that this was the period when the giant, plant-eating sauropod dinosaurs thrived!

« BRACHIOSAURUS »

At up to 30 metres long, dinos don't get much bigger than the Brachiosaurus (apart from Diplodocus, of course!). These sauropods were herbivores that swallowed their food (plants) whole as their teeth weren't pointy enough for chewing. Being so tall gave them a big advantage when it came to reaching high-up leaves.

The name 'Brachiosaurus' means 'arm lizard', because its front legs were longer than its back ones.

« DIPLODOCUS »

The infamous Diplodocus could reach up to 31 metres long. These beasts were nothing short of colossal! Diplodocus were herbivorous sauropods that walked on four legs. Their weapon of choice was their huge tail, which could whip away predators. In fact, their name means 'double beam', which describes the double row of bones supporting its gargantuan tail.

ALLOSAURUS

Ferocious Allosaurus was a great, big hunting dinos that could destroy and devour even the biggest sauropods. Allosauruses had big skulls, as well as colossal claws and razor-sharp teeth. These guys packed a serious punch! Allosaurus lived on a diet of herbivores, including Stegosaurus and Diplodocus.

'**Allosaurus**' means 'different lizard', due to its uniquely shaped spine.

They walked around on two legs and were about 12 metres long.

Large plates along its back and tail.

STEGOSAURUS

Stegosaurus was not the speediest mover, but its iconic spikes make it super-recognisable. The 9-metre-long armoured dinosaur had bony plates in two rows along its back. A Stegosaurus' tail had large spikes that would help defend it from dangerous dino predators.

Diplodocus could grow to be longer than three London buses put together. Woah!

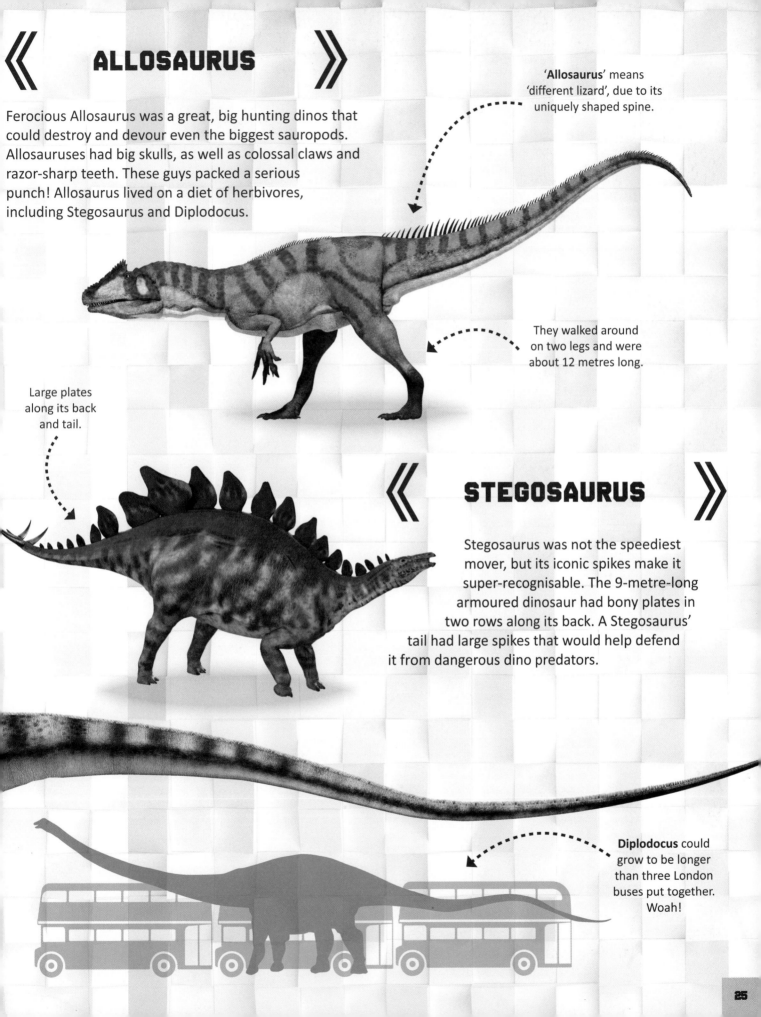

DIPLODOCUS

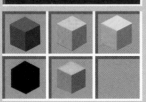

MATERIALS

Reaching for plants was a total breeze for the long-necked Diplodocus. Here's how to create your own.

The **Diplodocus** was the longest known dino!

+ STEP 1

Start by building the feet. Use a layer of blue blocks and then add four white claws.

+ STEP 2

For the leg, build up blue blocks as shown in the pictures. When you are happy with the shape, layer up the blocks in stages to make it look 3D.

+ STEP 3

Repeat steps 1 and 2 until you have four feet and legs. Make sure that they line up and that there is enough space between them for the large body (check step 4 for sizing). Now connect the back legs to the front using blue blocks, like this.

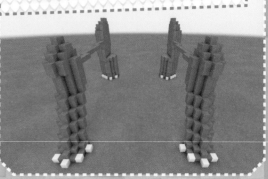

STEP 4

Continue making the frame by adding a row of blue blocks behind each of the two back legs, like this. This will eventually become the tail. Do the same thing from the front of the dino legs to start making the neck.

STEP 5

Add an arch of blue blocks to connect the two front legs. Build a second arch joining the back two legs. Finally, add a spine down the middle to connect up the two arches.

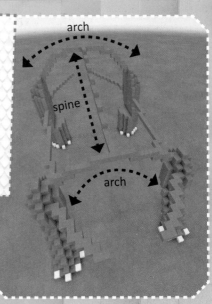

arch

spine

arch

STEP 6

Now use the frame to guide you as you fill in the body. Overlap the blocks to create a curved shape. We made the top half of our dino blue, and the underbelly cream.

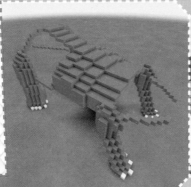

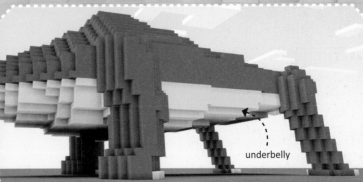

underbelly

STEP 7

Your Diplodocus now needs its iconic tail. Build a line of blocks from the back of its body. Then, build it up with more blocks to make it thicker. The underside should be cream and the top should be blue.

STEP 8

At the front of its body, add on a long, curved neck using a row of blue and cream blocks. Then, add more blocks in layers to make it thicker.

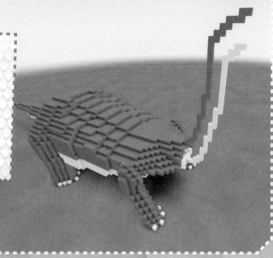

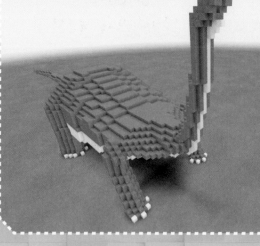

STEP 10

Give it yellow and black eyes. The blue blocks underneath the eyes should stick out more than the rest of its face to look a bit like cheeks.

STEP 9

Build your Diplodocus' head on the top of its long neck, like this.

STEP 11

Now all that is left to do is add the bottom jaw. Use a row of cream blocks for this bit. Take your time to get the nostrils and facial details just right. Finally, check that you are happy with the size and length of your dino. Done!

ALLOSAURUS

Check out our
fearsome Allosaurus,
then follow the steps
to create your own.

Don't get too close,
this dino bites!

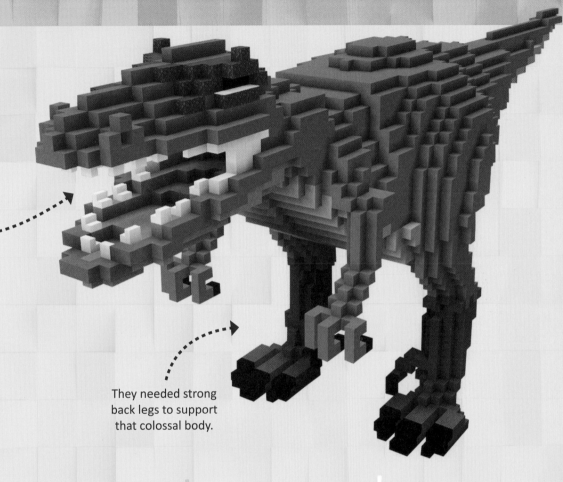

MATERIALS

They needed strong
back legs to support
that colossal body.

STEP 1

An Allosaurus needed
a good set of sturdy
feet to hold up that
hefty body. Use brown
blocks to create their
three-toed feet and
then add a second,
slightly smaller, layer.

STEP 2

For the leg frame, use
brown blocks nearest its
foot, then red blocks to
create the upper leg.

STEP 3

Next, fill in the frame
you've built to create
its two-toned leg.

STEP 4

The leg should be curved with a slight bend in the knee. Fill in the leg to give it some definition, like this. Repeat these steps to create another leg. Tweak them until you're happy with it.

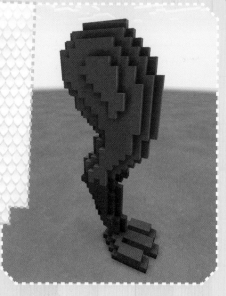

STEP 5

Now, add a brown claw on the inner part of each foot. Join up the legs with red blocks to form its hips, as shown.

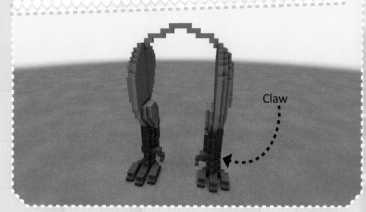

Claw

STEP 6

Use more red blocks to begin mapping out the Allosaurus' spine. It's best to start from the hips built in step 5, and then work your way outwards from there.

STEP 7

At the front of the dino, add an oval of red blocks, like this. This will become the base of the neck.

STEP 8

Create a net for the tail using two more rows of blocks. These should join up with the top of the legs. Fill in the net to make a solid tail. Next, build two more rows of blocks off the front of the legs to form a torso net.

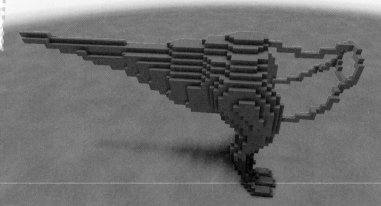

STEP 9

Grab plenty of red blocks to fill in the torso frame that you've built. Your Allosaurus should be looking like this!

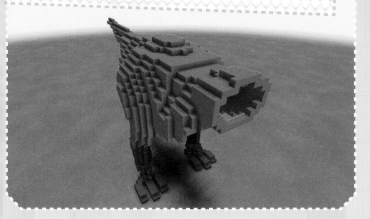

STEP 10

For the underbelly, add a line of pale orange blocks that reaches right the way down the body to the tip of its tail. Then, fill in the underside of its torso.

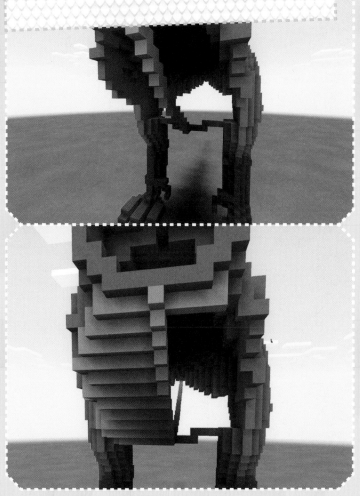

STEP 11

To flesh out the tail use pale orange blocks to create a two-toned effect, just like ours. Don't forget that Allosaurus tails are wide but not very long compared to some dinos!

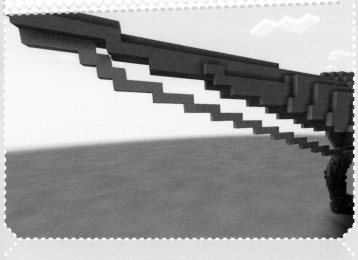

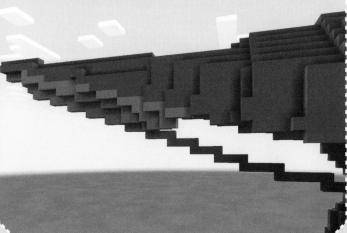

STEP 12

For the top of the dino's head, add a small arch of red blocks. Use the picture below as a guide for how the head should connect to the rest of your build.

STEP 13

Make an oval-shaped frame for the top jaw. It should join up with the tip of your dino's face and base of its neck, as shown.

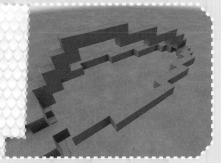

STEP 14

Give your dino an open mouth by adding in a bottom jaw. The frame should gradually extend downwards to create the open jaw shape.

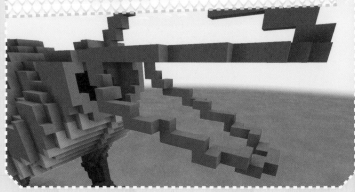

STEP 15

Use pale orange blocks under the jaw line for the dino's chin. This will connect up with the Allosaurus' underbelly.

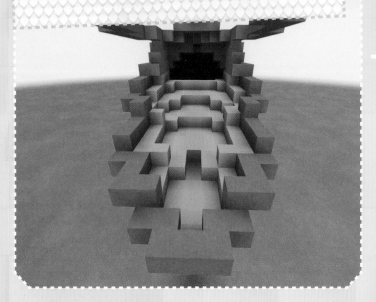

STEP 16

Use red blocks to form the top of the dinosaur's head. Look at the image for how to create layers, which get smaller the closer you get to the tip of its head. This will make its crest.

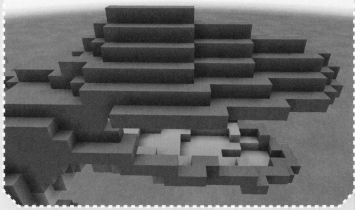

STEP 17

A couple of black blocks make the perfect set of terrifying eyes. Use textured red blocks around the eye area to give your Allosaurus' face some extra detail. Some yellow carpet under the eyes will help them to stand out.

STEP 18

Finish off the inside of its mouth with some bright pink blocks. Make sure you add them to the inside of both the top and bottom jaws.

STEP 19

To make the nostrils, build a little cave shape out of red blocks, as shown.

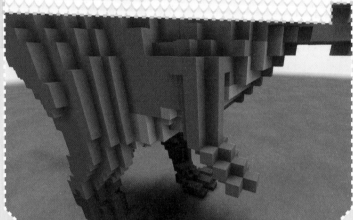

STEP 20

Up the fear factor by making a mouthful of bright white teeth! Add a row of blocks to the top and bottom jaw.

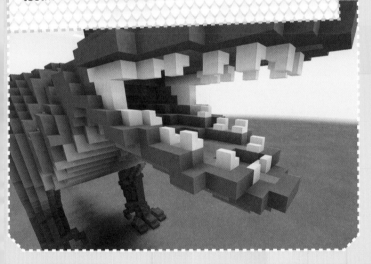

STEP 21

Add two red arms coming off the front of the dino's torso. Remember that Allosaurus' arms were quite short, so you don't need many blocks for these ones.

STEP 22

Build red feet with three toes on each end. Then, add a black block onto each to create the claws.

STEP 23

Keep hold of your black blocks so you can add some claws to finish off its feet.

STEGOSAURUS

Get ready to build the iconic Stegosaurus!

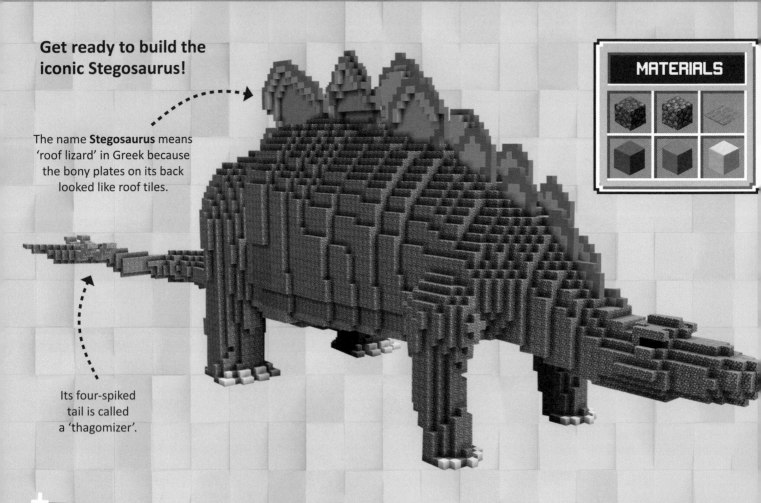

The name **Stegosaurus** means 'roof lizard' in Greek because the bony plates on its back looked like roof tiles.

Its four-spiked tail is called a 'thagomizer'.

MATERIALS

STEP 1

Build your first foot using textured green blocks. It should be rounded like this. Use five white blocks to give the foot claws.

STEP 2

Next, build a leg frame using the same blocks as the foot. Look at the picture to see how wide the ankle and leg parts should be.

STEP 3

Next, fill in the leg. Layer up the blocks to make it look 3D and muscular. The base of the leg is almost as wide as its foot.

STEP 4

Make another leg, using the picture to help you get the space between them just right. Then, join them together with a high arched shape. These should all be built with the same blocks.

STEP 5

You'll need plenty more of the green blocks to build the Stegosaurus' spine. Make sure it curves to mark out where the neck and tail should be.

STEP 6

Now, build outwards from the back of the legs to make a frame for the bottom of the torso. Look at the picture to see where it curves to make room for the back legs.

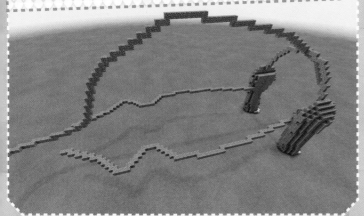

STEP 7

Make the frames for both of the back legs. The back legs should be a little taller than the front ones. Look back at the image of the finished build to help you get it just right.

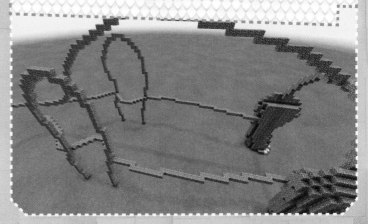

STEP 8

Fill in the back feet and add white claws. We made the claws look 3D by using two layers to create them, as shown in the picture.

STEP 9

Complete your Stegosaurus' two back legs by filling them in to make them 3D. Remember to experiment with layering to give them a rounded shape.

STEP 10

Now that your dino has four strong legs, it needs a torso. Start to fill in the area around the spine using the same colour blocks.

STEP 11

Build up the sides of your Stegosaurus' torso, too. Use the layering technique to create the curve of its body.

STEP 12

Keep filling in the torso with lots of blocks. Your build should really be taking shape now. Use the picture to help you make the legs blend in with the rest of the dino.

STEP 13

Next, add in a line of blocks for the underbelly. It should start at the neck and go right the way to the tip of its tail. Make a note of how close to the ground the underbelly line reaches.

STEP 14

At the back of your dino, have a go at creating a frame for its tail. Make sure it gets narrower towards the tip, as shown.

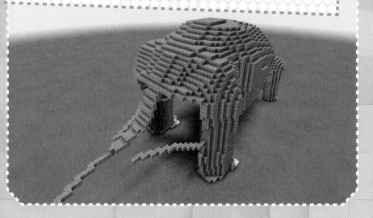

STEP 15

Fill in the tail base with your blocks, so that it gets smaller the closer it gets to the tip. Don't worry about getting it perfect first time – the more you experiment, the better.

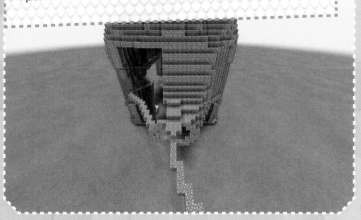

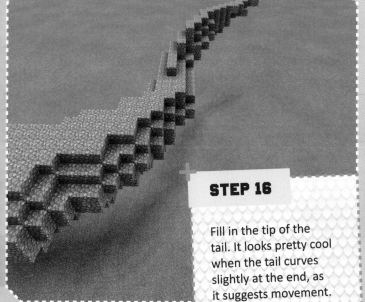

STEP 16

Fill in the tip of the tail. It looks pretty cool when the tail curves slightly at the end, as it suggests movement.

STEP 17

To bring the tail to life, add a super thin end that is a little further from the ground. You should be able to imagine it swishing around!

STEP 18

However, the tail is not done yet! Use purple blocks to create the fierce spikes on the tip of its tail. This will make your dino into a true stegosaurus.

STEP 19

At the opposite end of its spine, add a circle of blocks for the base of its head. Then, fill in the neck area completely so that it's ready for the next step.

STEP 20

Use the picture on the left to help you create a frame for the dino's head. It works best if your frame has one line coming from the top of its head to its nose, and then one on each side for its jaw.

STEP 21

Now fill in the head to get a strong 3D shape. The layers of blocks should get narrower towards the top of its head.

STEP 22

Knock out a couple of blocks on the side of its head to make space for some black eyes. Do the same on the opposite side. Try adding two blocks underneath the eyes, to make them stand out, as shown in the picture.

STEP 23

Grab some flowerpot blocks to make the nostrils. Take a look at the picture to help you to decide on the best place to put them.

STEP 24

It wouldn't be a Stegosaurus without the distinctive plates running along its back. We've used yellow blocks with an orange outline to make the plates stand out.

STEP 25

The spikes are smallest near the head and get larger towards the top of the back. Try making some of the larger plates 3D by adding a couple of extra rows of blocks along the top.

STEP 26

Add some grey blocks to make the end of the Stegosaurus' nose. Finally, use the same grey blocks to fill in its underbelly and chin. Your dino is complete! Why not experiment by making a smaller Stegosaurus in a different colour to create a dino family?

COOL
《 CRETACEOUS 》

The Cretaceous period occurred as the land continued to move apart, creating continents. A more recognisable planet Earth began to take shape. At this time, more varieties of dinosaurs existed than ever before. Dino species now had ample space to thrive, plus oodles of new plants and flowers to feed on.

Their enormous jaws were over one metre long.

《 TYRANNOSAURUS REX 》

Meet the most famous dino of all time! Tyrannosaurus Rex, or T. rex, as it is more commonly known, was a large theropod that walked on two legs. 'Rex' means 'king' in Latin. They were 12 metres long and carnivorous. They had a totally terrifying set of teeth that could grow up to 18 centimetres long. These teeth made light work of chomping through bone!

《 VELOCIRAPTOR 》

Any Jurassic Park fans out there will no doubt recognise this carnivorous dinosaur (even though they didn't actually live in the Jurassic period!). They moved on two legs and it is believed that they had feathers. They also had plenty of pointed, sharp teeth. Velociraptors were a pretty small theropod, measuring roughly 1.9 metres long.

ANKYLOSAURUS

Ankylosaurus was a type of armoured dinosaur, and one of the largest at that! Besides being covered neck to tail in plates, Ankylosaurus had a whopping clubbed tail to use as a weapon. The 7-metre-long creature walked on four legs and had a beak with big grinding teeth. You seriously wouldn't want to cross one of these!

Check out that clubbed tail (then make a quick getaway).

They had a big tummy with plenty of room for digesting all those plants!

It is thought that Iguanodons had very long tongues.

IGUANODON

The name 'Iguanodon' means 'iguana tooth' in Greek. These herbivores were 10 metres long and got around on both two and four legs. Iguanodon remains have been found all over the world, which is a sign of a super-adaptable dino.

Their big thumb spike may have been used to defend it from predators.

TRICERATOPS

You can recognise a Triceratops by its distinctive frill and three impressive horns. This scary looking plant eater had horns on its face for defending itself against hungry predators or fighting fellow Triceratops. They had pointy beaks and sharp teeth for chomping plants and could grow up to nine metres long.

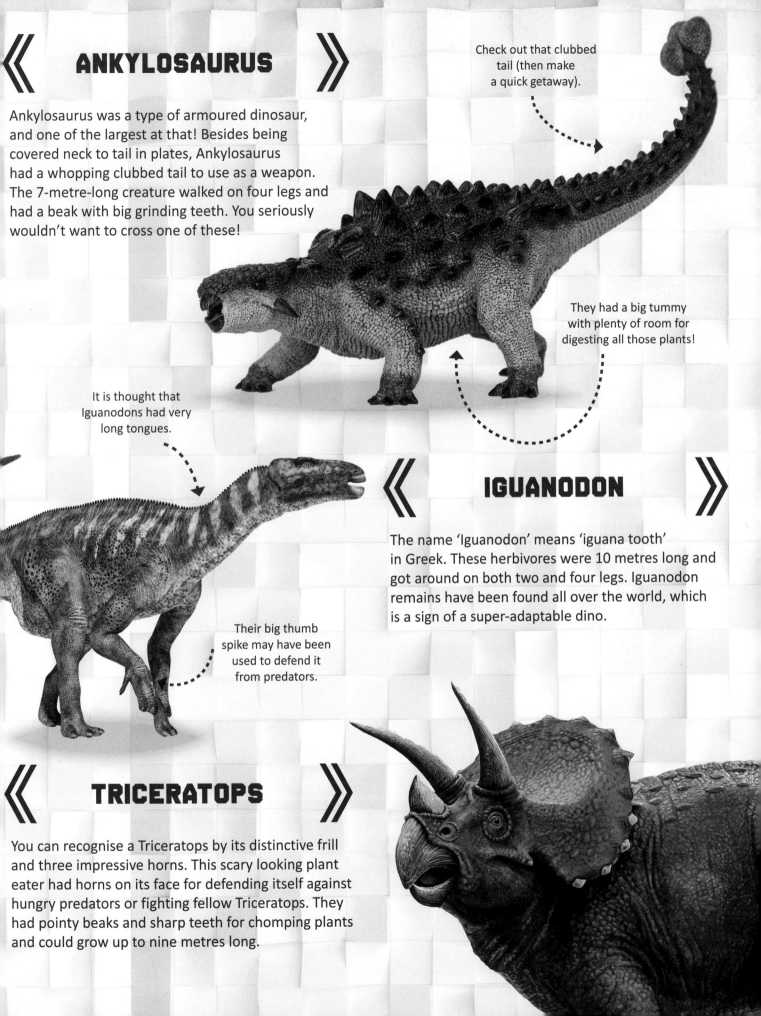

TYRANNOSAURUS REX

MATERIALS

Everyone loves a T. rex, and now you can build your own with these simple instructions. Rule your Minecraft world with the king of the dinosaurs!

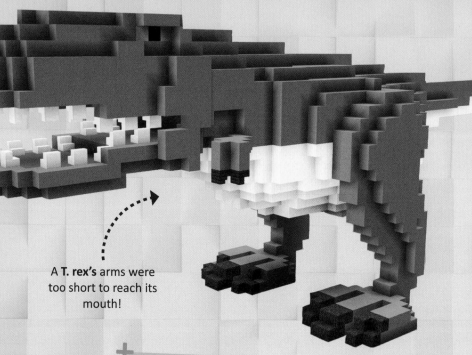

A **T. rex's** arms were too short to reach its mouth!

STEP 1

Start your T. rex by using brown blocks to build a three-toed foot, like this.

STEP 2

Form an ankle and then make the outline of the rest of the legs as shown below. Now, fill in the gaps and add a smaller three-toed foot on top to add shape.

STEP 3

Repeat the first two steps to make a second foot and leg, then join them at the top using a archway of blocks.

STEP 4

Make the shape of the spine by building a stepped diagonal line that's slightly lower at the back.

STEP 5

The T. rex's belly should reach about halfway down its legs. Build the outline as shown below, with the top of the belly on one level and a curve at the bottom.

STEP 6

Now build curved 'ribs' from the brown spine down to the top of the lighter-coloured belly. Make sure it's smaller towards the tail end.

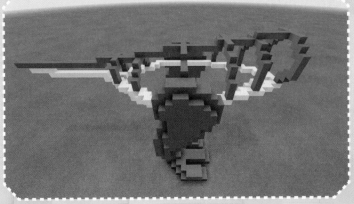

STEP 7

Fill in the belly and back in the correct colours, layering to ensure you give your T. rex a nice rounded shape.

STEP 8

Now add a line of blocks in a slightly different colour along the top of the spine.

43

STEP 9

For the arms, start with a few brown blocks on each side of its torso, like this. Remember that their arms are really short! Next, give each arm three fingers.

STEP 10

Map out the head by creating a net. Use dark green and black blocks to embed its green eyes in the sides of its head.

STEP 11

When you're happy with the shape of the head, use brown blocks to fill it in and make it solid. Then, add the bottom jaw beneath it, like this.

STEP 12

Fill in the inside of the mouth using dark pink blocks, and add lots of those all-important white teeth.

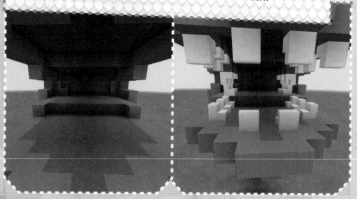

STEP 13

Finish your T. rex with some dark brown blocks to make claws. You are now done!

ANKYLOSAURUS

Monochrome blocks at the ready for making this dino!

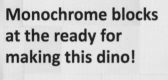

kylosaurus had a horny beak and leaf-shaped small teeth

STEP 1

Begin by arranging grey blocks in a big foot shape, like this.

MATERIALS

STEP 2

Use grey blocks to create a frame for the leg.

STEP 3

Next, build up the outside of the leg so that it forms a solid shape. Layer the blocks in a graduating pattern to make the leg look 3D.

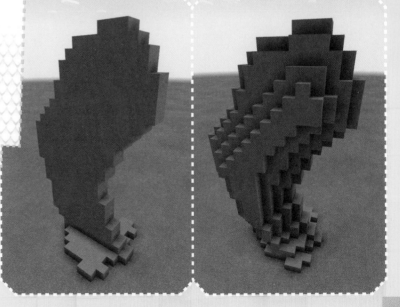

STEP 4

On the inside of your build, fill in the inner leg until you reach half way up. Repeat steps 1-4 to build the second leg.

STEP 5

STEP 5

To join up the legs, build a band of grey blocks between the two, as shown. Check out the picture below to help you work out how far apart the legs should be.

STEP 6

Now it's time to build a frame for the body. First, add a curved strip of blocks in front of the band that you built in step 5. Now build a rectangular shaped torso, plus a triangle tail.

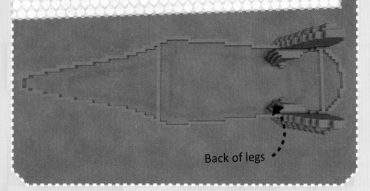

Back of legs

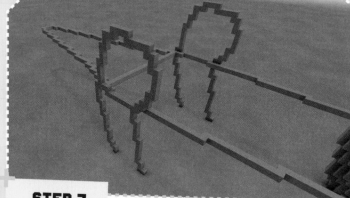

STEP 7

Using the front legs as a shape and size guide, have a go at building a frame for the dino's back legs. When you're happy with it, begin filling in the outline.

STEP 8

Keep building up the back legs until they are as detailed as the front ones. Your dino is beginning to take shape. Awesome!

STEP 9

Next, it's time to map out the shape of the torso. To start, build grey arches between the two back legs, then between the two front ones. Build a spine from the front of its torso to the tail.

STEP 10

Develop the frame of your dinosaur by building bands of grey blocks right the way along the torso. Use this image as a guide for how to position each part of the frame.

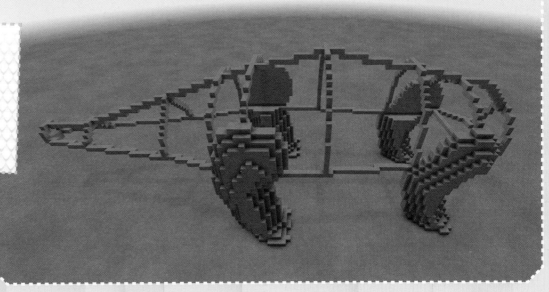

STEP 11

Hope you've got plenty of grey blocks, because you're going to need them! Fill in the frame you've made by layering them up, like this. Don't worry about creating the underbelly just yet!

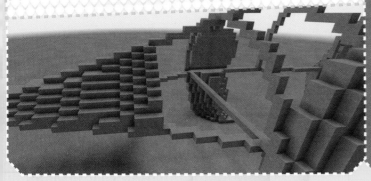

STEP 12

Create the large tip of its tail by making a fat heart shape, as shown.

STEP 13

Next, make a frame for the tip of the tail. Add a row of blocks above and a row below the frame you made in step 12.

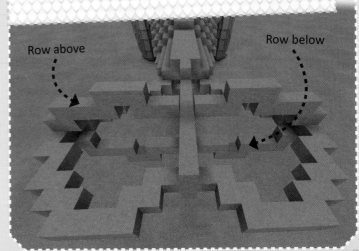

Row above

Row below

STEP 14

Fill in the frame of the tail by layering it up with grey blocks. Add two rows of blocks on top to make this dino's famous spikes.

STEP 15

Start forming the Ankylosaurus' pointed head by creating a simple triangular frame, as shown below.

STEP 16

From the tip of the point, begin to build the top of its head. It should look a bit like a set of stairs.

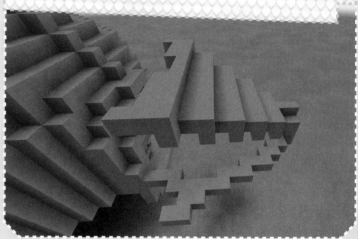

STEP 17

Now you can fill in the sides of the head. Make sure that the neck is filled in, too!

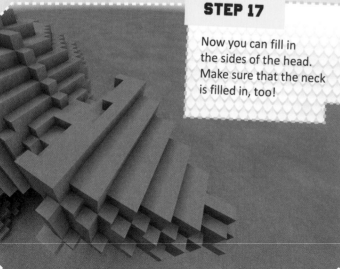

STEP 18

Place one black eye on each side of its head. Complete the eye area with a few purple blocks. This type of detail will set your dinosaur apart from all the rest.

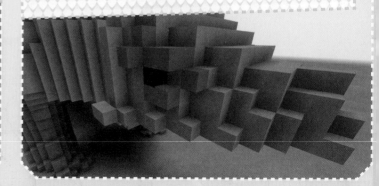

STEP 19

Use pale grey blocks to fill in the whole of your Ankylosaurus' underside. Don't forget to fill in the tail too!

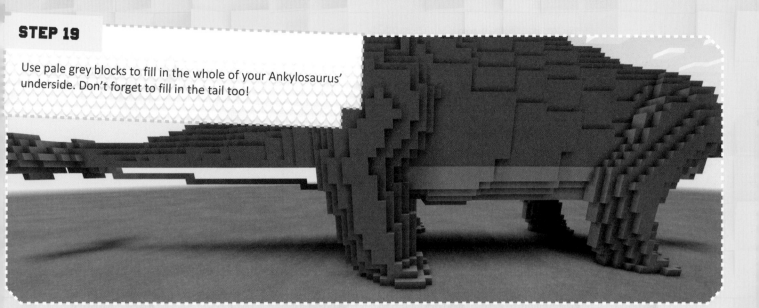

STEP 20

To decorate the face, try using some dappled grey and white blocks. It looks awesome when arranged in rows like this.

STEP 21

Then, use the same dappled blocks to decorate along the dino's back. We've created clusters of these blocks for more impact.

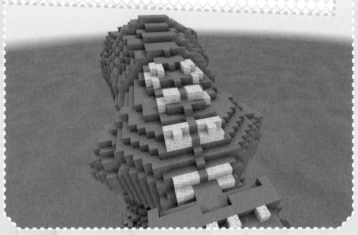

STEP 22

To finish your build, carry on with this technique right the way along the top half of its body and down its tail.

TRICERATOPS

MATERIALS

It's Triceratops time! How will your three-horned dino turn out?

Sharp beak for chomping plants!

The frill may have protected their neck.

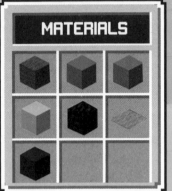

STEP 1

Make the first foot using brown blocks. Then, create claws with two layers of white blocks.

STEP 2

Next, build up the leg frame with brown blocks, as shown here. Repeat this so that you have two.

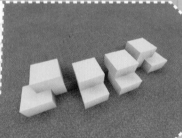

STEP 3

Fill in the two legs, then connect them up with a tall arch of blocks. The top of the arch will be the top of its back.

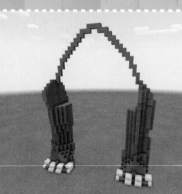

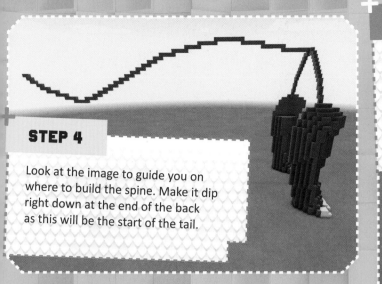

STEP 4

Look at the image to guide you on where to build the spine. Make it dip right down at the end of the back as this will be the start of the tail.

+

STEP 5

Create a frame for the torso and chest. This is how your build should look from above.

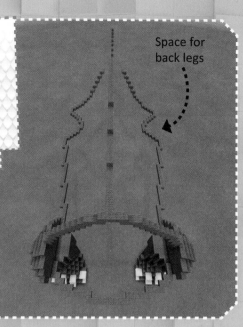

Space for back legs

STEP 6

It's time to build the frames for the back legs. They should be the same shape as the front ones. Remember, they should slot into the indents that you created in Step 5.

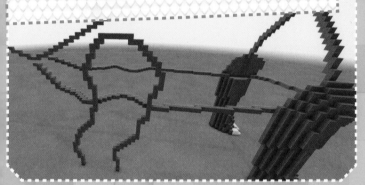

STEP 7

Begin by flat-filling the back legs, so that they are still 2D shapes. This will help with the following steps.

STEP 8

Build the two back feet at the bottom of the back legs. They should be the same shape as the front ones. Pop on white blocks for claws.

STEP 9

Build up layers of brown blocks to build the two sturdy back legs. You should end up with a 3D shape.

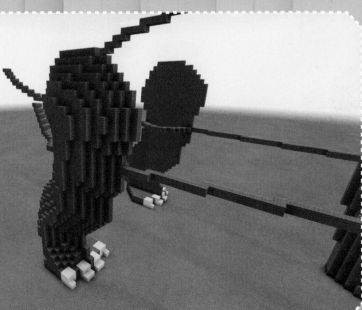

51

Begin filling in the area around the spine, as shown. Then you will be ready to move onto filling in the rest of the torso.

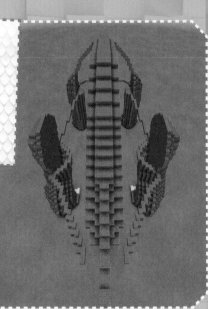

STEP 10

To complete the Triceratops' torso frame, add in a line of brown blocks that reaches right down the centre of the build. This will become the dino's underbelly.

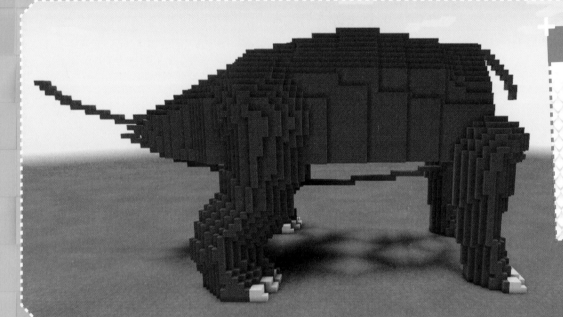

STEP 12

Next, you'll be needing more of your brown blocks to build up the sides of the Triceratops' body. Once you have made the dino as wide as you need to, you can build the sides straight down so that they appear flat.

STEP 13

To get the dino's tail shape just right, simply add an extra row of brown blocks to it, as shown here.

STEP 14

Create a circle of brown blocks to map out the base of the head. Then, build a row of blocks sticking out from the bottom of it, as shown. This will become the bottom of its head and chin area.

STEP 15

Look carefully at the below picture for how to make the head frame. We've built in an outline for the bottom jaw, plus another line for the shape of its forehead and snout.

STEP 16

Now you can start to fill in the top of its head and snout area. Gradually add layers of blocks so that it begins to look a bit like a staircase. This will make your head 3D.

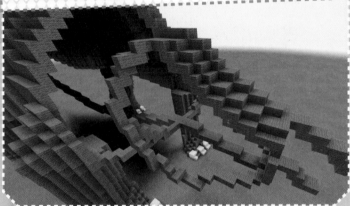

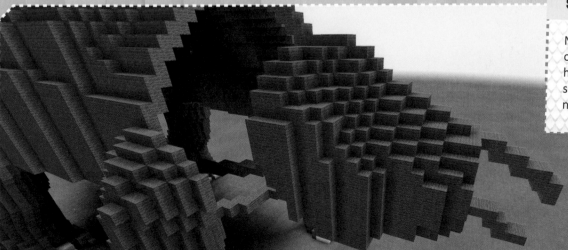

STEP 17

Now it's time to move onto the sides of its head. Remember that it should become narrower near the nose area.

STEP 18

Now it's time to begin building the horns!
Use a pale brown colour for the base of each one.

STEP 19

Use white blocks to build up the horns until they look like this. Notice how the nose horn isn't very long at all.

STEP 20

Your dino needs some eyes. Pop in some black blocks so that they're underneath each horn. Give them a light brown outline and then add a couple of grey carpet blocks beneath.

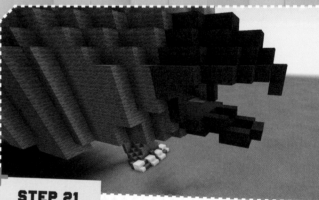

STEP 21

Use dark brown blocks to create its beaked mouth. We have designed ours so that it looks open. Try adding an extra block to the tip of the top section to make it look pointed.

STEP 22

For the underbelly, use light brown blocks until there are no gaps right the way along the torso.

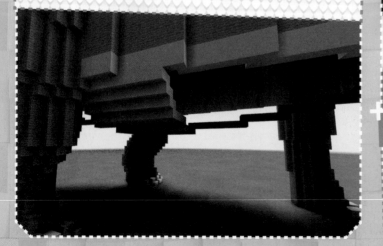

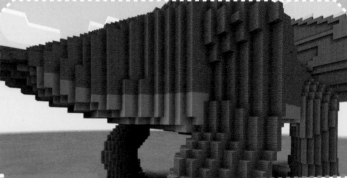

STEP 23

Use the underbelly line as a guide for filling in the Triceratops' tummy. Use your light brown blocks (the same as the ones you used around its eyes) for this stage.

STEP 24

Fancy adding some jazzy detail to your build? Knock out some existing blocks along the line where the underbelly meets the brown sides and replace them with the opposite colours to create a gradient, as shown below.

STEP 25

Create a fan of five spikes around the head. This is the beginning of the frill.

STEP 26

Next, build a ring around these spikes to outline the frill.

STEP 27

Now fill in the neck frill with lots of brown blocks. You could recreate the patterns that we've built into ours, or experiment with a different pattern.

STEP 28

For a finishing touch, use a handful of white blocks to add little details along the tips of the Triceratops' frill. Then, do any final tweaks to make your dino perfect!

《 SKY AND SEA 》

Some of the coolest prehistoric creatures that ever lived dominated the sea and sky throughout the Mesozoic Era. From the Pterodactyl to the Mosasaurus – how many do you recognise and which will you build?

《 PTERODACTYL 》

These impressive dinos, with their goblin-like features, are Pterosaurs. They are flying reptiles. Their scientific name is Pterodatylus, which means 'winged finger'. Despite being a classic dino character, these flying reptiles were not technically dinosaurs.

《 MOSASAURUS 》

Look at those jaws! These aquatic lizards ruled the seas during the Cretaceous period and were called Mosasaurus. The seriously hefty hunters could reach 15 metres long. They hunted for turtles, large fish and smaller Mosasaurus near the surface of the water – a bit like crocodiles do today.

Their powerful tails would help drive them through the water.

ARCHAEOPTERYX

These feathered carnivores lived near lagoons and hunted in shallow water. They were pretty small in dinosaur terms, at just 0.5 metres long, and lived in the Jurassic period. They were quite bird-like and either flew or walked on two legs – Archaeopteryx were fast runners! Unlike modern beaked-birds, Archaeopteryx had teeth.

PTERANODON

This toothless dino is called a Pteranodon, which means 'wings and no teeth'. They existed during the late Cretaceous era, living in flocks and hunting for fish. They were unique-looking with large beaks and a large crest on top of their heads.

 ## DIMORPHODON

The medium-sized Dimorphodon was a Pterosaur. Its name means 'two-form tooth' because its fang-like teeth grew in two different sizes. It was quite a strange looking creature, with its large head and long tail, and it lived during the Jurassic period.

PTERODACTYL

MATERIALS

Follow the instructions to make your own perfect Pterodactyl!

These reptiles had around 90 short, spiky teeth.

STEP 1

Before you start, remember that this build needs to be off the ground, so it looks as though your dino is flying. Use pale purple blocks to make a shape like this. This will be the length of its body.

STEP 2

Then, add another strip of blocks that crosses over the first strip in the middle. The crossover should be slightly off-centre, as shown below.

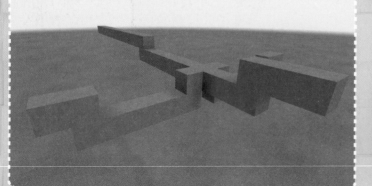

STEP 3

Next, add more pale purple blocks to fill in its body in a flat, circular shape. From above it should look like this.

STEP 4

Use the blocks to create a point at the front of the body. This will eventually become the dino's neck.

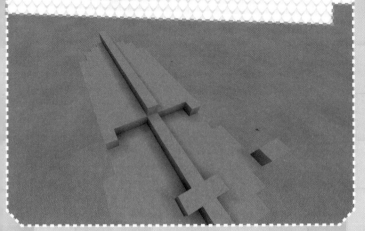

STEP 5

Grab some dark purple blocks and use them to build an arched shape from the front to the back, like this.

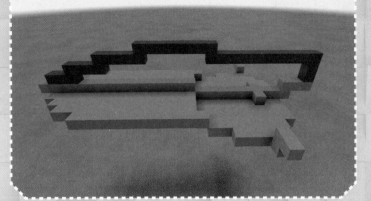

STEP 6

Create a net to map out the dino's large wingspan. Be sure to give each wing a pointed tip. It works best if your wings are symmetrical!

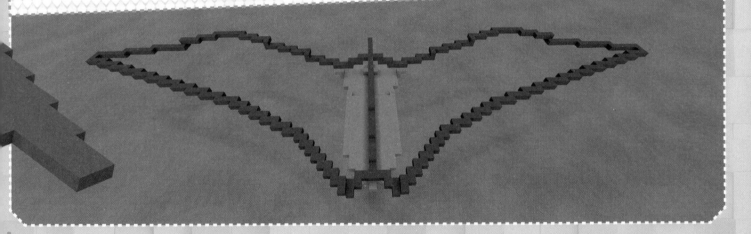

STEP 7

Now it's time to fill in the torso and wings with plenty of dark purple blocks! Make your build look more realistic by adding extra layers of blocks to make it 3D. Step the blocks gradually to form the shape of your dino.

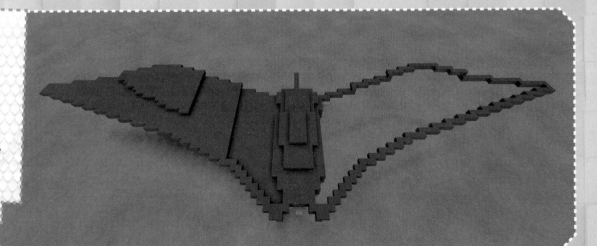

STEP 8

Use pale purple blocks to give your Pterodactyl its back feet complete with three claws. They should connect to the back of its body, as though pushed out behind it.

STEP 9

Use pale purple blocks to make the front claws. These should be joined to the front of the wings.

STEP 10

Build out the neck, like this. Use pale purple blocks for the underside and dark for the top part of the neck.

STEP 11

Create an open jaw by adding a row of steps going down from the neck. Build a flat oval shape straight out, like this.

STEP 12

Give the dino its enormous crest by building diagonally backwards. At the base of the crest, add yellow blocks for eyes.

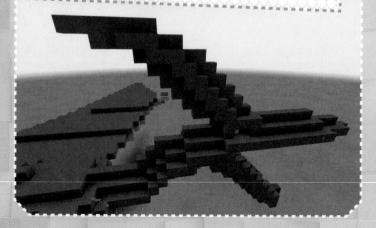

STEP 13

Finish your dinosaur by filling in the jaw, adding a pink tongue and some glistening white teeth. You're ready to take off!

ARCHAEOPTERYX

Make a feathered friend with ferocious features that's sure to impress!

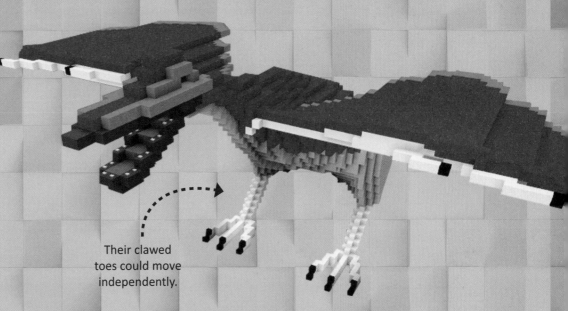

Their clawed toes could move independently.

MATERIALS

STEP 1

Like most of our dino builds, it's best to start with the feet. Use white blocks to make three long toes. The base of the foot is pretty small.

STEP 2

For the leg, continue with the white blocks. Make them lean back on an angle, like this. Repeat these steps to make the second leg.

STEP 3

Add a few grey blocks around the top of each leg, as shown here. This will become the base for your dino's body.

STEP 4

Create 2D upper legs with grey blocks by looking at the picture on the right. Make sure that you build them on an angle to create a bend in the leg.

STEP 5

You should now have two matching legs, like below. Now join them both up with a little arch made out of the same grey blocks.

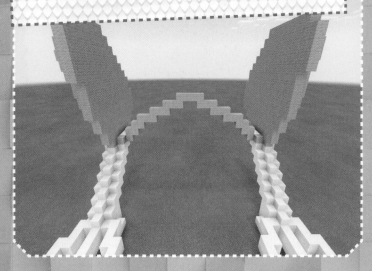

STEP 6

Make the upper legs look more realistic by building them up with layers of grey blocks. We think three layers works well to get a sleek 3D shape.

STEP 7

Add a row of grey blocks coming out from the middle of the arch that you built in Step 5. This will make your dino's chest. Then, build a frame for its back with blue blocks. Connect this to the top of the arch from Step 5.

STEP 8

Now you can begin filling in its back with more blue blocks. Keep going until both sides are filled in completely.

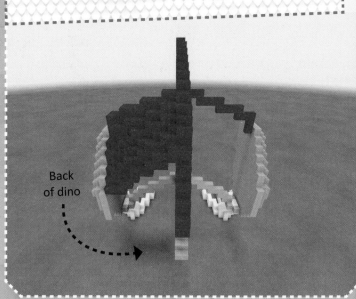

Back of dino

STEP 9

At the front of the dinosaur, create a frame for the rest of its torso, and its neck. Look at our picture to see how it gets narrower towards the neck end. Then, join up all the rows of blocks by building a small circle at the end.

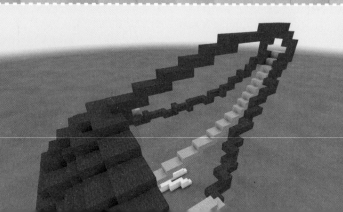

STEP 10

Keep filling in the top half of the frame, from the neck to the back. This is how your build should look from above as you fill in any gaps!

Back of dino

STEP 11

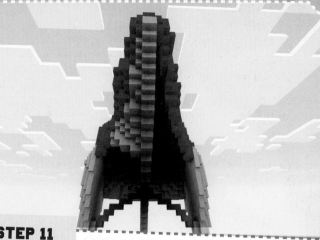

At the front of your Archaeopteryx, begin adding grey blocks to fill in the underside of its torso. Continue adding more grey blocks to get a 3D shape.

STEP 12

Once you reach the back of the Archaeopteryx, it's time to fill in its hips. The underside of the legs should be curved, as shown below.

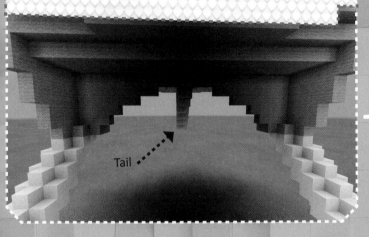

Tail

STEP 13

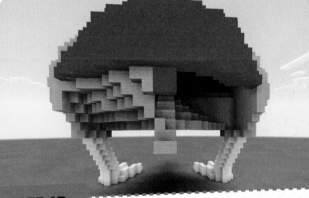

Then, fill in its lower back. The image shows how the dinosaur looks when this step is halfway through.

STEP 14

Use more blue blocks to mark out the top of the head. This is where your build gets interesting!

STEP 15

Add a bit of colour variation with some bright blue blocks. Use these to fill in the face shape and add more detail. Don't forget to mark out where the eyes will go by creating an eye socket on each side, too.

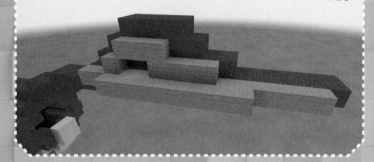

STEP 16

Finish making a frame for your dino's neck by adding a row of grey blocks underneath the existing blue one.

STEP 17

Create an open beak with a darker shade of blue block. Take a good look at the image below for how to create a stair-like lower jaw. Take your time to get the angle just right.

STEP 18

Using the same blue blocks as the top half of the torso, build a simple wing frame. Look at the finished image to see how wide to make the wings.

STEP 19

Fill in the enormous wings. Use dark blue for the main section and then add a row of bright blue blocks to create a border. Finally, add in some pink blocks for a tongue.

STEP 20

To make wing tips, add white blocks in a staggered formation. Then, add black blocks for its claws on both its legs and wings.

STEP 21

At the back of your dinosaur, build a frame for its huge tail using the same blue blocks as the wings. Don't underestimate the size of the tail – they were pretty big!

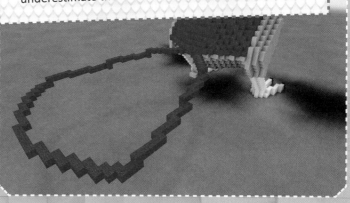

STEP 22

When you've got the shape how you want it, begin filling in the tail using a combination of blue coloured blocks. Use the bright blue blocks to highlight the tail design.

STEP 23

For its teeth, use small yellow blocks, like these. They should be dropped along the line of the blue gums.

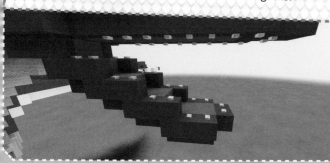

STEP 24

Your dinosaur is complete. Take some time to admire your jaw-dropping Archaeopteryx and make any tweaks you want.

MOSASAURUS

You'll need all your best building skills to tackle this water-dwelling Mosasaurus! When it's done, we'll show you how to create its home.

MATERIALS

STEP 2

Next, begin to form the top of its head. Create a curve using a row of purple blocks, like this. This line will help you to form the dinosaur's head and face.

STEP 1

As this dino swam around underwater, make sure that it isn't touching the ground. Start by building a frame for its torso and head.

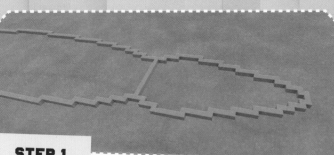

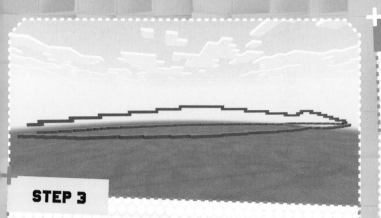

STEP 4

Next, add on a curved tail with a pointed tip. Don't forget to look at our picture of the finished build to double check the scale if you need to.

STEP 3

Continue adding to this row of purple blocks to map out the shape of its body. Can you see how it dips just after the head? This will become the neck.

STEP 5

Now, you can fill in the top half of your dino's torso using tonnes of purple blocks. When you're done, simply add another row of purple blocks for the underbelly frame. This new row should join up with its tail.

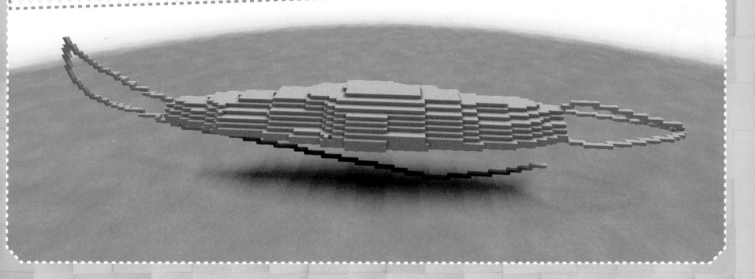

STEP 6

Develop the frame for your Mosasaurus tail. Add rows of purple blocks to make it 3D, then begin to fill it in until it's completely solid with no gaps.

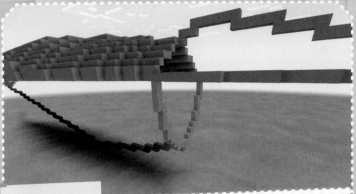

STEP 7

Now move back over to the front end of your build. Make a semi circle of turquoise blocks that connects up to each side of the body, as well as to the underbelly that you built in Step 5.

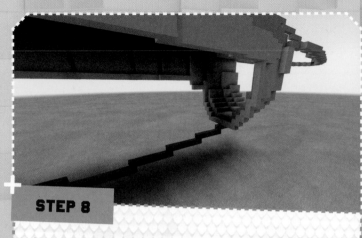

STEP 8

Use turquoise blocks to start to fill in the underside of your build. This will create a distinctive two-tone effect for your dino. Keep going until the whole torso is filled in, right up to the neck.

STEP 9

This is how your build should look now that you've filled in the torso and tail. This is a good chance to take a look at how your build is shaping up, and make any tweaks that you need to.

STEP 10

Use this image as a guide to help you to create a frame for your dino's face. The frames should gradually step upwards towards the top of the head.

STEP 11

Continue to build up the top half of the head. You should be aiming for a shape a bit like the above. Don't forget to leave an eye hole on each side of its head.

STEP 12

Give your dino an eye using a black block or two. Then, frame each eye using dark purple blocks, like an eyelid. Some turquoise carpet helps make them stand out!

STEP 13

Build out the lower jaw so that its mouth is wide open. Most of the jaw should be turquoise, with a row of purple blocks to show the line of its mouth.

STEP 14

To finish off the enormous mouth, you'll need some pink blocks. Make sure that the top and bottom has a layer of pink, connecting in the middle.

STEP 15

Use white blocks to make a set of terrifying teeth. Use pale purple blocks to build a tongue. We made ours stick out a little further than the bottom teeth.

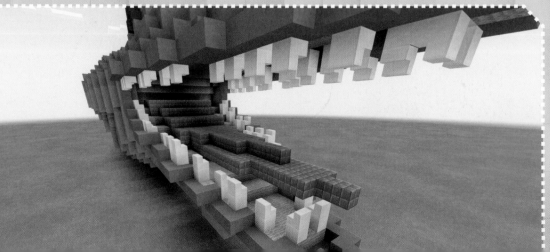

STEP 16

Use purple blocks to build four frames for the four fins, then fill them in. Check out the picture on the right to see how we joined it to the torso.

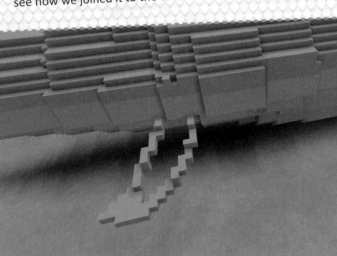

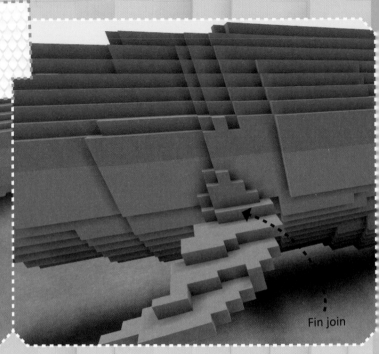

Fin join

STEP 17

Grab some dark purple blocks and add a row of them right the way along its back. We used the same purple blocks as we did above the eyes in step 12.

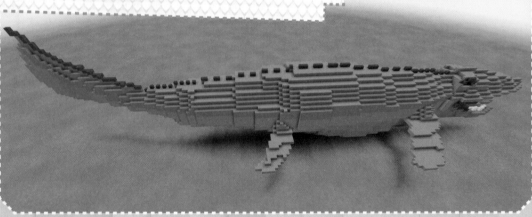

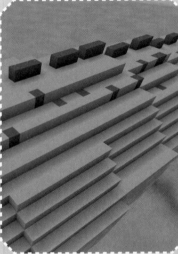

STEP 18

Looking to add some extra detail to your creation? Have a go at knocking out a few blocks along each side of its torso where the blue and purple meet.

STEP 19

Look at the below image for how to fill in the gaps you just made. By blending the two colours you create a gradient effect. Now your dino looks even more realistic!

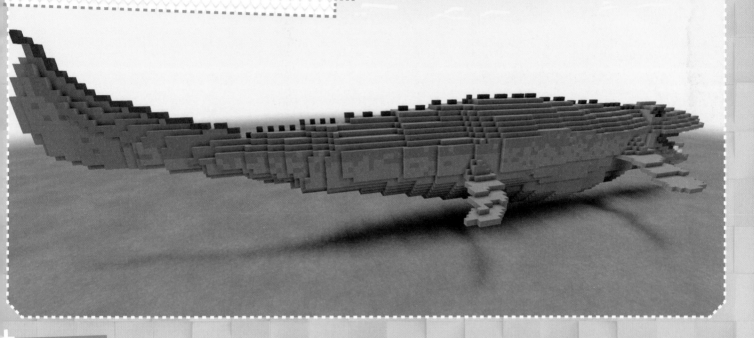

STEP 20

Why not experiment with adding water? Try adding sea lanterns to illuminate your Mosasaurus after dark.

DINOSAUR
« FAMILIES »

When the Maiasaura dinosaur was first discovered, it made us question everything we knew about dinosaur behaviour and relationships!

« DINO COMMUNITY »

Some scientists believe that these dino communities would protect and feed their young until they were ready to start their own family. When remains of prey is found near a nest, it suggests that the dino parents would have been bringing their babies food.

« DINOSAUR BABIES »

In the 1970s, a Maiasaura nesting site of fossilised eggs, babies, and adult dinos was found. This suggested that the dinosaurs lived together in groups and raised their young. Up until this point, people didn't think that dinosaurs were sociable!

Since the discovery of the **Maiasaura** nesting site, similar ones have been found all around the world.

This one is a modern reconstruction.

IS IT TRUE?

There is a lot of debate about these dinos! While some believe that Maiasaura were born helpless, relying on their parents, many think that they were more independent than this.

The dinos were named **Maiasaura**, which means 'good mother lizard'.

MAIASAURA

Things are about to get serious. Supreme Master serious!
Do you think you're ready to take on the Maiasaura and
her trio of youngsters? There's only one way to find out.

MATERIALS

STEP 1

Start with a baby
Maiasaura. Build its
back foot with three
toes using purple
blocks. Use the same
colour blocks to build
a flat leg shape, like
this.

STEP 2

Build up the bottom
section of the leg
using layers of blocks.
Next, add a ring of
purple blocks to build
the top of the leg.

STEP 3

Make the leg 3D by adding layers of purple blocks on each side. Repeat this to build the other back leg.

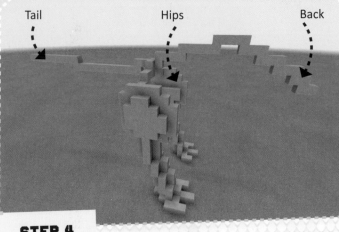

Tail   Hips   Back

STEP 4

Build a bar of blocks for its hips to join up the top of the two legs. Then, give it a spine by copying the row of blocks in the picture above.

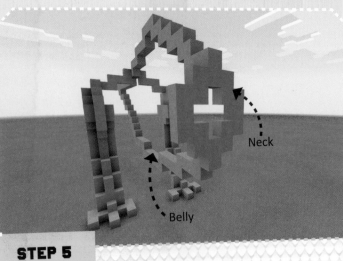

Neck

Belly

STEP 5

Look at the picture for how to build the front of the dinosaur. Add a row of purple blocks underneath the spine to create a frame for its belly. Then, add in a circle for its neck, like this.

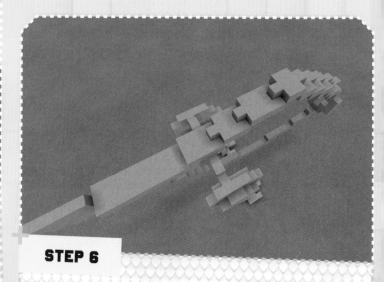

STEP 6

It's time to start filling out the dino's back. Do this by building outwards from its spine using plenty of purple blocks.

STEP 7

Check out the picture for how to get the frame for the tail in the just the right position.

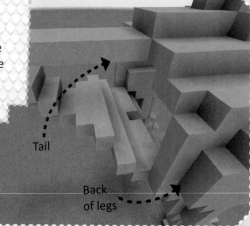

Tail

Back of legs

STEP 8

Fill in the frame that you built in Step 7 to make it 3D. Take note of how the tail is wider at the base.

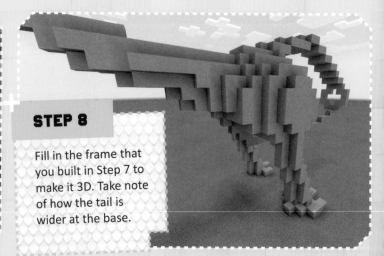

STEP 9

Once you've filled in the tail and base, continue filling in the torso and the area around the back legs.

STEP 10

Continue layering up your purple blocks, like this, until the entire torso is filled in right up to the neck.

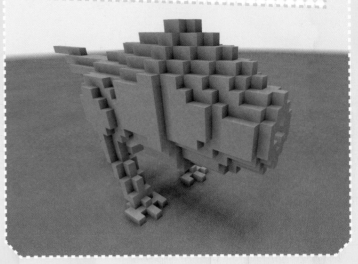

STEP 11

Your Maiasaura is missing its front legs! Start by creating a simple leg shape, like this, with a three-toed foot at the base, and a 2D leg.

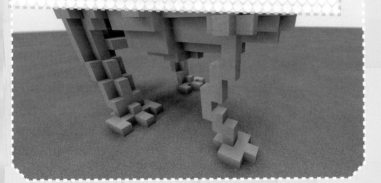

STEP 12

When you've built two front legs, you can add in more details to give the legs definition – just like you did for the back legs.

STEP 13

It's a good idea to create a frame for the dino's head. Start with the jaw and forehead.

STEP 14

Fill in the top half of its head using purple blocks in layers. Then, build a frame for the bottom jaw and fill this in, too.

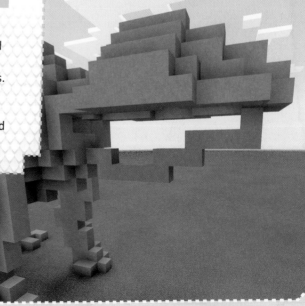

STEP 15

Knock out some purple blocks all over the dino's body. Then, fill in the holes with orange blocks. This dino is starting to look realistic!

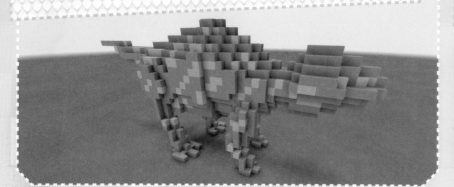

STEP 16

Use a black block for each eye. Then, frame them with dark purple blocks, like this.

STEP 17

Did you enjoy building the young Maiasaura? Why not have a go at making it some brothers and sisters? Try to put them in different poses, too.

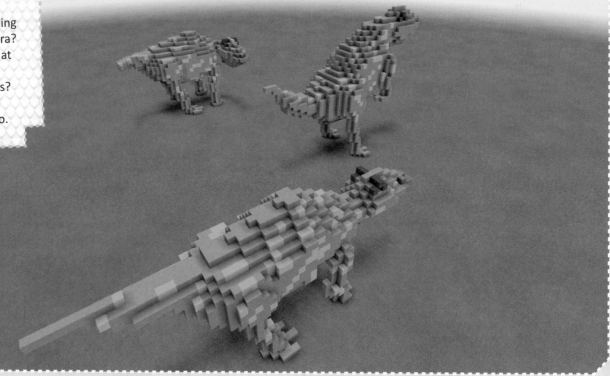

STEP 18

Make a little dino who is standing up tall by making its back legs long and straight. Try to tilt its torso, as well.

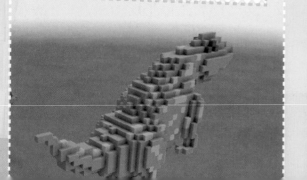

STEP 19

Have a go at building one of your dinos so that they are twisting their head sideways, like this chap.

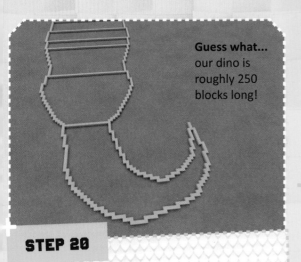

Guess what... our dino is roughly 250 blocks long!

STEP 20

Planning is essential when you're building the Maiasaura mother. Create a frame for its huge tail and the end of its torso, using the picture above to help you.

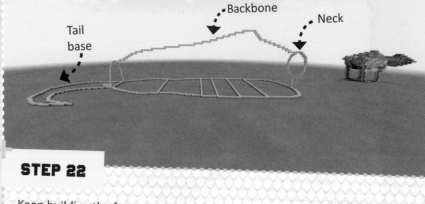

Tail base

Backbone

Neck

STEP 22

Keep building the frame until it looks like this. Build an arch of grey blocks for the tail base. At the front of the dino, build a stalk with a circle on top for the neck. Then, add in a row of grey blocks to map out the backbone, which connects the tail base with the neck.

STEP 22

Now, start building up the base of the frame using grey blocks.

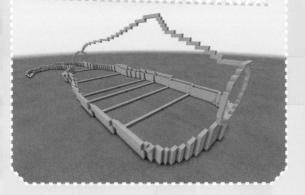

STEP 23

Look at the picture for how to build up the frame. Take note of where to change to dark grey and purple blocks in your layering.

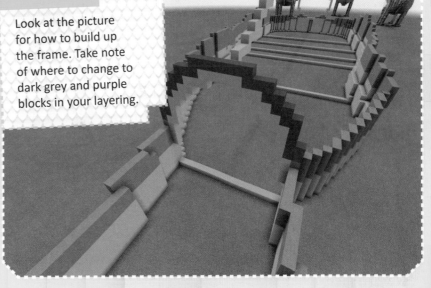

STEP 24

Continue to layer up your dino using lots of purple blocks to create the back and top of the torso.

STEP 25

Keep going until the torso looks like this. Make sure that your dino has a hump about halfway down its back.

STEP 26

Now, move onto the tail. Remember that Maiasaura have thick tails.

STEP 27

Extend the frame for the neck using purple and grey blocks. Use the picture to help you create the shape.

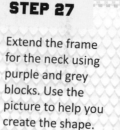
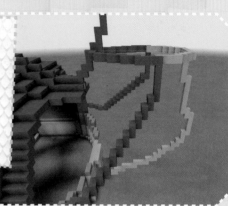

STEP 28

Fill in the dino's chest with grey blocks, as shown. Then, create a purple frame for its upper jaw and the top of its head.

STEP 29

Fill in the dino's head by building up layers of purple blocks. Give the dino a black beak, which is slightly open, like this.

STEP 30

For the eyes, use regular black blocks. Add grey carpet blocks underneath. Use some extra blocks around each eye to make eyelids.

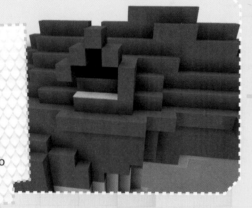

STEP 31

Create a frame for both back legs. Follow the shape shown in the picture to make them bend correctly.

STEP 32

When you're happy with the shape of the back legs, fill in the details. Build them up with grey and purple blocks to make them 3D.

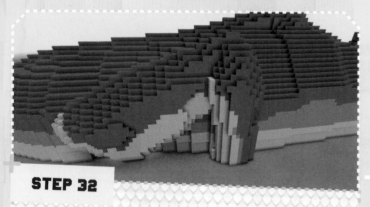

STEP 33

Finish off each back leg by building a purple foot with three chunky toes, as shown.

STEP 34

Give your Maiasaura its front legs. They should also be bent as your dino is lying down. Use these images to help you with each stage of the front legs.

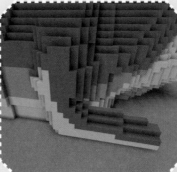

STEP 35

Use these pictures as a guide for how to add the yellow and green patterns on the dino's skin. Knock out a cluster of blocks, then fill in the gaps with irregular shapes using yellow and green.

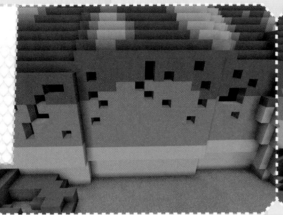

STEP 36

You've made it to the end. Zoom out and make any last tweaks! Then take a bow, you've earned it!

GLOSSARY

ARMOURED
Medium sized dinosaurs with tough scales that protected their bodies.

BIPEDAL
Walking on two legs.

CARNIVORE
Meat-eating animals.

CRETACEOUS
Geologic period from the end of the Jurassic to the start of the Tertiary.

FLOCK
Group of animal that travels, rests or eats together.

HATCHLINGS
A creature that is newly hatched from an egg.

HERBIVORE
Animals that only eat plants.

JURASSIC
Geologic period from the end of the Triassic to the start of the Cretaceous.

THEROPODS
Diverse group of meat-eating dinosaurs that walked on two legs and had short arms.

TRIASSIC
The period of time after the Permian era, and before the Jurassic period began.

PTEROSAUR
Flying reptile that lived alongside the dinosaurs. Became extinct at a similar time.

SAUROPOD
Large, four-legged dinos with long necks and a plant-based diet.

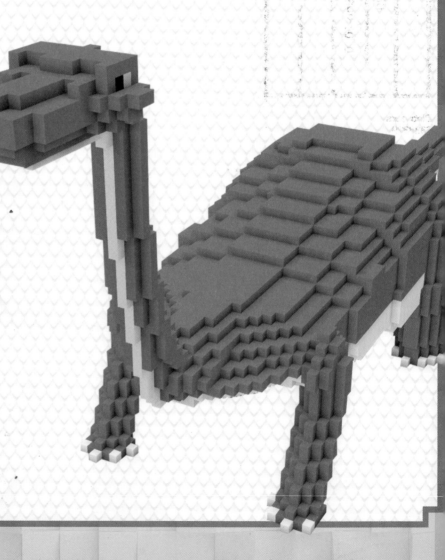